Getting
the Picture

A Brief Guide to Understanding
and Creating Visual Texts

Getting the Picture

A Brief Guide to Understanding and Creating Visual Texts

Marcia F. Muth

University of Colorado at Denver

Karla Saari Kitalong

University of Central Florida

Bedford / St. Martin's   Boston ◆ New York

For Bedford/St. Martin's
Developmental Editor: Beth Castrodale
Production Editor: Kendra LeFleur
Senior Production Supervisor: Dennis Conroy
Editorial Assistant: Caryn O'Connell
Production Assistant: Amy Derjue
Copyeditor: Cynthia Benn
Text Design: Claire Seng-Niemoeller
Cover Design: Donna Lee Dennison
Composition: Ewing Systems
Printing and Binding: R.R. Donnelley & Sons Company

President: Joan E. Feinberg
Editorial Director: Denise B. Wydra
Editor in Chief: Karen S. Henry
Director of Marketing: Karen Melton Soeltz
Director of Editing, Design, and Production: Marcia Cohen
Managing Editor: Elizabeth M. Schaaf

Manufactured in the United States of America.
9   8   7   6   5   4
f   e   d   c   b
For information, write: Bedford/St. Martin's, 75 Arlington Street, Boston, MA 02116 (617-399-4000)

ISBN: 0–312–41850–7

Acknowledgments

   Figure 1.1: Front page, *USA TODAY*. Copyright © May 16, 2001. Reprinted with permission. Front page, *The Wall Street Journal*. Reprinted by permission of *The Wall Street Journal*, copyright © 2003 Dow Jones & Company, Inc. All rights reserved worldwide.
   Figure 1.3: Article, *Forbes* magazine. Reprinted by permission of *Forbes* Magazine, copyright © 2003 Forbes Inc. Photograph on left by Jonathan Olley/Network, courtesy of Corbis. Photograph on right by Mark Jenkinson, courtesy of Corbis. Article, *Parenting* magazine, June/July 2003. Photograph, courtesy of Corbis.
   Figure 1.4: Design by Studio InFlux / The Art Institute of Boston at Lesley University: Jenny Barrett, ManChing Cheng, Lisa Goode, Yehudit Massouda.
   Figure 1.14: Web page copyright © 2003 Office of Community Service Learning. All rights reserved.
   Figure 1.19: Web page copyright © 2003 Smithsonian Institution.

Acknowledgments and copyrights are continued at the back of the book on page 50, which constitutes an extension of the copyright page. It is a violation of the law to reproduce these figures by any means whatsoever without the written permission of the copyright holder.

Preface for Instructors

Because students live in a highly visual world, they need to learn how to examine the visual documents around them and how to create their own documents — ones that meet the needs of, and even inspire, their audience. This supplement introduces the critical tools to do both.

The first part of the booklet, "Strategies for Designing Your Document," offers basic guidelines for formatting papers, integrating images, and using other design elements to create rhetorically sound and visually effective documents. The second part of the booklet, "Strategies for Understanding Visual Representations," helps students to read visual texts — advertisements, photographs, and other images — and think critically about them.

The skills that this booklet builds are required today in both the college classroom and the workplace. To mention just a few examples, the booklet can be used in courses such as these:

- Any composition course where students are expected to submit clear and effectively designed papers and other documents
- Courses with a special emphasis on visual analysis or the creation of visual texts
- Service-learning courses in which students create brochures, newsletters, posters, Web sites, or other documents with visual elements
- Business-writing courses that emphasize the importance of creating documents that meet the needs of prospective employers and customers

Key Features

Based on chapters from the sixth edition of *The Bedford Guide for College Writers* by X. J. Kennedy, Dorothy M. Kennedy, and Sylvia A. Holladay, this supplement provides clear explanations with plenty of examples to help students understand and apply the concepts covered. Specifically, it includes these class-tested components:

- Thorough coverage of the major principles of effective document design
- Advice for creating visually sound documents, illustrated through examples as varied as research papers, résumés, *PowerPoint* presentations, magazine articles, Web pages, and brochures
- Strategies for using three levels of visual analysis to "read" an image, covering (1) the identification of its context, purpose, and audience;

(2) the literal description of its characteristics; and (3) the interpretation of its meaning based on the feelings, moods, cultural associations, and themes it evokes

- Lively photographs, ads, and periodical extracts to illustrate visual elements and engage students in visual analysis

- Introductory checklists that help students consider purpose and audience for both documents they are designing (Part 1) and visuals created by others (Part 2)

- Concluding checklists that help students create documents using major features of effective design (Part 1) and analyze the major visual elements used in others' images and visual documents (Part 2)

- Thought-provoking exercises for both document design and visual analysis, including suggestions for group work

These features are designed to help your students analyze the images they encounter and to apply visual principles successfully in their own texts — in short, to get the picture!

Acknowledgments

We wish to thank all of the users and reviewers of *The Bedford Guide for College Writers* who helped to shape the document-design and visual-analysis features included in that book. We also thank Scott Orme of Spokane Community College, who helped us figure out how to make the material work effectively in a stand-alone supplement. His comments and suggestions were extremely valuable. In addition, we appreciate the insights of our students — Karla's at the University of Central Florida and Marcia's at the University of Colorado at Denver in her writing workshop, sponsored by the School of Education.

At Bedford/St. Martin's, we are deeply grateful to Joan Feinberg, who saw the need for this booklet and whose instincts and ideas have been invaluable. We'd also like to thank Leasa Burton, who helped bring the booklet from concept to reality and who was a source of many good ideas along the way. We extend warm thanks as well to the editors of the sixth edition of *The Bedford Guide* — Michelle M. Clark, Maura Shea, Amanda J. Bristow, and Genevieve Hamilton — who helped shape the innovative visual analysis chapter. As the editor of this booklet, Beth Castrodale helped to refine the visual features further and to find new materials. Caryn O'Connell tenaciously tracked down additional visual examples and assisted with permissions. Finally, we are grateful to Kendra LeFleur for ably managing the production process under a tight deadline and to Marcia Cohen and Elizabeth Schaaf for their invaluable production expertise and support.

Marcia F. Muth and Karla Saari Kitalong

Contents

CHECKLISTS

FIGURES

Introduction for Students

C hances are that on any given day you are bombarded by images of all
kinds. Before you even arrive at school or work, you pass billboards,
flashy storefront advertising, and signs of all types. Even the cars in front of
you have bumper stickers with slogans and logos. Walking to class, you pass
fliers pasted to poles, colorful posters on bulletin boards, and people reading papers displaying the day's headlines.

That's only the beginning. As the day progresses, you take in all kinds
of images — Web pages, work documents, product assembly diagrams, television programs and ads, newspaper stories, magazine articles, and photographs. Probably, you don't even notice — *really* notice — much of what
you see every day. In some respects, that's a good thing; your mind's filter is
at work, keeping you from being overwhelmed by the images, colors, and
words competing for your attention. But at many times, being especially
aware of visual information pays off on both personal and practical levels.
Your awareness helps you to make better sense of your world and your reactions to the images around you. It makes you a more critical consumer,
student, or worker. Ultimately, it helps you make better decisions because
you are better informed about the power of what you see.

This visual awareness is a skill and, like any other skill, it takes practice.
This booklet is meant to give you such practice. It discusses — with plenty
of examples and exercises — not only major strategies for analyzing visual
information but also useful principles for designing your own documents
for college, work, and other settings. Developing your visual awareness will
prepare you to apply such principles in your college classes and to turn
in documents that are both visually and verbally effective. It also will prepare you to consider purpose and audience in your workplace documents,
designing communications that meet the expectations of co-workers and
customers.

Part 1 of this booklet, "Strategies for Designing Your Document," offers
basic guidelines for formatting papers and using images. It briefly introduces design elements to help you create documents that are both rhetorically sound and visually effective. Part 2, "Strategies for Understanding Visual Representations," will help you to read visual texts — advertisements,
photographs, and other images — and think critically about them.

We hope that this booklet begins a closer engagement between you and the visual world around you. We hope, too, that it encourages you to think of yourself as a "document designer"—someone who can bring an understanding of the visual world to the creation of documents and who can communicate with, and even inspire, readers.

Part I
Strategies for Designing Your Document

Whether the document you prepare is an essay, a research paper, or a business letter, creating an effective design for it helps you achieve your purpose and meet the expectations of your audience. Through your own reading, you may have noticed that you respond differently to documents depending upon their appearance. For example, look quickly at Figure 1.1. Which of the two newspapers there seems more appealing to you?

If you prefer *USA Today*, you're like many Americans—you like the look of a colorful, casual newspaper and may even consider it easier to read. But if someone asked which of the two newspapers seems more credible or trustworthy, many would say the *Wall Street Journal*. Its closely typed text, narrow columns, and limited use of color create a look more "respectable" than that of the open, friendly *USA Today* with its abundant pictures, more colorful design, and playful tone. As you can see, the same features that make the *Wall Street Journal* seem more credible than *USA Today* may also make it less inviting to read. Like other newspapers, however, the *Wall Street Journal* freely uses headlines, short paragraphs, column dividers, white space, page numbers, and other visual markers that help the reader grasp the structure of the text at a glance and decide where to plunge in. Without such visual markers, the pages of the *Wall Street Journal* would provide the reader few pathways into its content.

Occasionally, college students are assigned a composition that looks and reads like a newspaper. But most of the papers you will write are not as visually complex as the *Wall Street Journal* or *USA Today*. Instead of calling for multiple columns, headlines, and graphs, your teacher will most likely expect to see double-spacing, one-inch margins, numbered pages, and indented block quotations—visual markers typical of college compositions. Figure 1.2 shows two pages—the first page and the list of sources—of a typical college composition that follows the guidelines of the Modern Language Association (MLA).

1

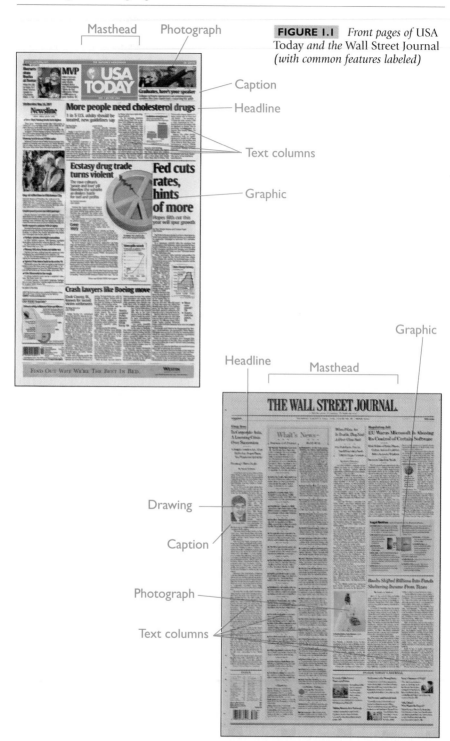

Masthead   Photograph

Caption

Headline

Text columns

Graphic

FIGURE 1.1   *Front pages of* USA Today *and the* Wall Street Journal *(with common features labeled)*

Graphic

Headline   Masthead

Drawing

Caption

Photograph

Text columns

FIGURE 1.2 *The first page and Works Cited page of a student research paper in MLA format*

1″

½″
Goers 1

Writer's last name and page number

Sarah E. Goers — Writer's name
Professor Day — Instructor's name
English 101 — Course
28 January 2001 — Date

½″ or 5 spaces

Is Inclusion the Answer? — Title, centered

Inclusion is one of the most passionately debated issues in public education today. Full inclusion, defined as placing all students with disabilities in general education classes, has three main components: the integration of special education students into the mainstream classroom, educational planning and program-ming, and the clarification of responsibility for appropriate instruction (Heinich 292). Although the intent is to provide the best care for all children

general education
in the field beli
disabled childrer
not be in the bes
student. Disablec
from a general ec
school is prepare
if placed in a so
met due to low fu
a lack of necessa
suffer. For thes
inclusion over pa
programs are ques

1″

Double-spacing throughout

1″

Citation with author's name and page number in parentheses

1″

List of works cited on a separate page

1″
Works Cited

Centered heading

½″
Goers 10

Block, Martin E. "Did We Jump on the Wrong Band wagon? Problems with Inclusion." Palestra 15.3 (1999). 10 Oct. 2000 <http://www.palestra.com/Inclusion.html>.

Gaskins, Jacob. "Teaching Writing to Students with Learning Disabilities: The Landmark Method." Teaching English in the Two-Year College 22.2 (1995): 71-76.

Heinich, Robert, ed. Educating All Handicapped Children. Englewood Cliffs, NJ: Educational Technology Publications, 1979.

Hewett, Beth. "Helping Students with Learning Disabilities: Collaboration between Writing Centers and Special Services." The Writing Lab. 25.3 (2000): 1-4.

Jacobson, Linda. "Disabled Kids Moving into Reg-ular Classrooms." Atlanta Journal 5 May 1994: C1.

Mushard, Mary. "Special Schools Fall Victim to Inclusion." The Sun. 13 June 1993: B1.
½″ NewsBank. Boston Public Lib. 15 Jan. 2001 <http://www.newsbank.com>.

Radebaugh, Barbara. "NEA vs. AFT." Education 201-002 Lecture. William Rainey Harper College, Palatine, IL. 21 Jan. 1999.

Rios, Denise A. "Special Students Joining Regular Classrooms." Orange County Register 9 June 1994: A24. NewsBank. Boston Public Lib. 16 Jan. 2001 <http://www.newsbank.com>.

List alphabetized by author's last name

First line of entry at left margin

Subsequent lines indented ½″ or 5 spaces

3

Understanding Four Basic Principles of Document Design

Four key principles of document design will help you to produce effective documents in and out of the classroom. Use the following questions based on these principles to help you plan an appropriate design for your college papers or other documents:

PURPOSE AND AUDIENCE CHECKLIST

____ Who are your readers? What are their key concerns? How might your document design acknowledge their concerns?

____ What form or genre do readers expect? What features do readers see as typical characteristics of that form? What visual evidence would they expect or accept as appropriate?

____ What problems or constraints will your readers face? How can your document design help to address these constraints?

____ What is the purpose of your document? How can your document design help you to achieve this purpose? How can it enhance your credibility as a writer?

PRINCIPLE 1: KNOW YOUR READERS

Whether you are writing an essay for class or preparing an entirely different type of document, identifying your audience is a good first step toward creating an effective design. For most papers that you write in a first-year composition course, your primary reader is your teacher and your secondary readers include your peers. For some assignments, you might be asked to include other readers as well.

Suppose you've written a paper explaining the benefits of a longer school year to a real-world audience. An audience of parents would have different concerns than an audience of community leaders or of school officials or teachers. Teachers, for example, would need to be assured that their paychecks would keep pace with the longer work year. The school board would need to be convinced that the increased costs for salaries, building operations, and transportation would pay off in higher student achievement. And other community leaders might want to know how such a move could affect community safety, traffic congestion, and seasonal employment rates.

In deciding how to design your document, you might consider ways to acknowledge, even highlight the key concerns of your particular audience, perhaps using headings, white space, and variations in type style. You might also consider whether your audience is likely to read every word of your ar-

Quote emphasized   Photograph   Text columns

Text column   Photograph   Quote emphasized

FIGURE 1.3   *Common features in magazine design: page spread from* Forbes, *April 2, 2001, (top) and* Parenting, *June/July 2003 (bottom)*

gument or to skim it for key points. Perhaps visuals, such as tables, graphs, or diagrams, would make information more accessible. Thinking about such issues as you plan and draft means you'll have a better chance of reaching your audience.

PRINCIPLE 2: SATISFY YOUR READERS' EXPECTATIONS

When you think about a newspaper, a particular type of publication comes to mind because the newspaper is a familiar *genre*, or form. As Figure 1.1 (p. 2) shows, almost all newspapers share a set of defined features, such as a masthead, headlines, pictures with captions, graphics, and articles arranged in columns of text. Even if specific details of the form vary, newspapers are still recognized as newspapers. Similarly, *Forbes* and *Parenting* both belong to the genre of the magazine: both feature glossy pages, articles arranged in columns, notable quotes set in larger type, and photographs. Despite significantly different content, magazines share a common genre identification, as Figure 1.3 (p. 5) illustrates.

Like the newspaper and the magazine, the college paper can be thought of as a genre. Readers, including your teacher and your peers, have expectations about what topics are appropriate for such documents, how they should be written, and how they should look. Readers also have expectations about appropriate visual evidence, such as graphs, tables, photographs, or other illustrations, depending on the field and the assignment. Check your course syllabus to see whether your instructor requires a specific document design.

Usually your readers expect your paper to be word-processed with numbered pages. Other conventions may also be expected. Some teachers want you to include a cover page with your name, the title of your paper, your course number and section, the date, and perhaps other information. Others may prefer that you follow the MLA paper format, simply supplying a four-line identifier and a centered title on the first page (see Figure 1.2 on p. 3). Some will ask you to include your last name or a shortened title with the page number at the top or bottom of each page.

Unless your teacher encourages unusual or creative formatting, don't experiment too much with the appearance of a college paper. In fact, you can easily apply expected features to your papers by creating a template to use for all papers with the same specifications. First, format your paper the way you want it to look. Then, create a document template that you can access any time you begin a new paper. Depending on your word processor, you will follow a sequence like the following:

1. Create a duplicate copy of your formatted file.
2. Delete all of the text in the document.
3. Save the file as a document template.

4. Give the template a name, such as "English paper" or "Paper form."
5. When you create a new file, choose this template from the options in your template folder.

Although you should follow any specific guidelines that your instructor supplies, some genre features are flexible. For example, you might use a larger, boldface font for your paper title or use underlining or boldface to set off any headings. Perhaps you might want to separate your page numbers from the rest of the text with a horizontal line or insert a little extra white space between paragraphs. Such features could help to make your standard paper distinctive and easier for your teacher to read.

PRINCIPLE 3: CONSIDER YOUR READERS' CONSTRAINTS

Your teacher probably expects you to print your paper in a crisp, black, 12-point-size type, double-spaced, on one side of a white sheet of paper with one-inch margins. You also may be asked to reprint a paper if your toner cartridge is nearly empty. Before accusing your teacher of being overly picky, remember that he or she may read and grade compositions in batches of a hundred or more. Papers that are printed clearly in a standard format are easier on the eyes than those with faint print or unusual formats. In addition, your teacher needs sufficient margin space for comments. If you try to save paper by using a smaller font, narrower margins, or single spacing, the paper may be more difficult to read and harder to grade.

When you address readers besides your teacher, they too will have some constraints. Some may read your document on a computer screen if it arrives as an e-mail attachment. Others may skim a text's main points during the morning commute or sort through a stack of résumés before lunch. Just as you want to write an effective paper that addresses your readers' information needs, you also want to design a usable, readable paper — one that readers can readily absorb regardless of constraints.

PRINCIPLE 4: REMEMBER YOUR PURPOSE

Like most writers, you have in mind a particular theme, argument, or point of view that you want to convey to your readers. As you consider your readers' concerns, their expectations, and the conditions under which they read, your challenge is to take your readers' needs into account and to write convincingly for them. When you do so, you also increase your credibility as a writer.

Good document design is no substitute for a clear and well-organized essay, but it can help you achieve your purpose or reason for writing. The rest of this chapter will explain how to use document design to enhance the message you are trying to convey.

Creating an Effective Design for Your Document

When you design a document, you use tools such as typography, lists, white space, headings, repetition, and visuals. Although you may not be accustomed to thinking about design issues, you already make design choices whenever you type something in your word processor. *Typography* refers to the appearance of typeset letters on a page. When you put something in boldface type, use all capital letters, or change type size, you are making a typographic choice. Such choices can make your document clearer and more attractive, but inappropriate or excessive use of an option can clutter your work. The following guidelines can help you design effective documents that achieve your purpose and appeal to your audience.

USING A PROMINENT ELEMENT

Artists and designers aim to attract readers' attention by giving important elements prominence. Consider Figure 1.4, for example, which shows two panels of a six-panel brochure that was designed by a student. The image of the mannequin on the brochure's cover immediately draws the eye, but the pattern of light guides readers to the central question: "Is your life out of control?" Other words on the left panel (such as "broken," "scared," lost," and "depressed") serve as a suggestive backdrop, but there is no mistaking the main message.

Providing a prominent element helps your readers focus on what you think is most important. As you begin work on any visual document ask, "What is the main message I want to get across?" Once you have decided on that message, think of ways to give it prominence. For example, if you are designing a brochure, flyer, poster, or postcard, you might want to use one large headline surrounded by a significant amount of space, as the designer of the brochure did. Note also the effective use of headings in the right panel of the brochure. The headings — all questions — are parallel in form. They also appear in color for emphasis, and they are separated by white space so that readers clearly see the breaks between topics. (For more on white space, see p. 16; for more on headings, see p. 18; and for more on color, see p. 24.) The inside panels of the brochure respond to the questions posed in the headers, pointing readers toward resources where they can get help.

You can get ideas about how to present prominent elements by looking at visual documents designed by others. Learning to spot these elements — and figure out how they are given prominence — can also help you analyze and interpret visual documents. (For more information, see Part 2, p. 33.)

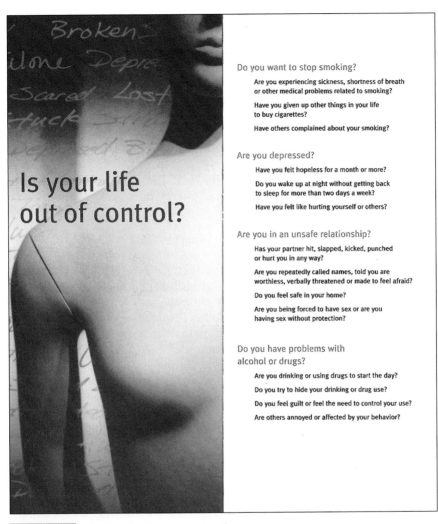

FIGURE 1.4   *Design showing prominent elements*
Source: Art Institute of Boston

CHOOSING FONTS

Current word-processing software allows you to change typefaces, commonly called *fonts*, to increase readability, achieve special effects, add emphasis, or set a particular tone in your writing. Although most college papers use a conventional font in a 12-point size, sometimes you may need to use larger size type for signs, posters, and visuals (such as *Power-Point* slides) for oral presentations. Test such materials for readability by printing samples in various type sizes and standing back from them at the distance of your intended audience.

Figure 1.5 shows the same sentence written in four different 12-point fonts: Times New Roman, Courier New, Arial, and Comic Sans MS. Although the examples are all written in the standard 12-point size, the typefaces occupy different amounts of horizontal space on the page.

Serif or Sans Serif Fonts.   Times New Roman and Courier New are called *serif* fonts. A serif font has small tails, or serifs, at the ends of the letters. Arial and Comic Sans MS, in contrast, are categorized as *sans serif*—without serifs. These fonts have solid, straight lines and no tails at the tips of the letters. You can see the difference between a serif and sans serif font in these examples:

Times New Roman (serif) B b C c   Arial (sans serif) B b C c

Sans serif fonts have a clean look, but they are less readable than serif fonts, especially in long passages. If you look over your local newspaper, you may notice a combination of serif and sans serif fonts. Typically, sans serif fonts are used for headlines and other display type, such as advertisements and "pull quotes" (interesting quotations that are "pulled out" of an article and printed in larger text to catch the reader's eye). On the other hand, most newspapers choose serif fonts for their article (or "body") text. In fact, Times New Roman, which is the default font on many word processors, was developed for *The Times* newspaper in London for its own use. Other common serif fonts include Palatino and New Century Schoolbook. A combination of fonts can provide the maximum readability and emphasis, as Figure 1.6 shows.

If you decide to combine two different fonts, keep these points in mind:

FIGURE 1.5   *Space occupied by different typefaces*

Times New Roman	An estimated 40 percent of young children have an imaginary friend.
Courier New	An estimated 40 percent of young children have an imaginary friend.
Arial	An estimated 40 percent of young children have an imaginary friend.
Comic Sans MS	An estimated 40 percent of young children have an imaginary friend.

Watching TV with a Critical Eye

By second grade, kids have figured out, often from personal experience, that the toys they see in commercials don't always measure up in real life. Children this age are old enough to get into more sophisticated discussions about fact and opinion. [. . .]

FIGURE 1.6   *Sans serif heading used with serif body font*
Source: Kiplinger's, *February 2000*

- Serif and sans serif fonts can be combined in the same document, though document designers recommend using only one of each.
- For further emphasis, you may vary the type size or type style, such as italics or bold, for each font.

Novelty Fonts.   For most college and professional writing, novelty fonts — those that are unusual or decorative — are inappropriate. **Comic Sans MS** is a novelty font, as are *Brush Script* and **Tempus Sans**. While these casual, playful typefaces may suit some writing situations, novelty fonts can set the wrong tone for your paper, especially if your subject matter is either very technical or very serious.

For example, if you are writing a paper about civil liberties, Comic Sans MS might suggest that readers don't need to take your arguments seriously or that you lack respect for a serious subject. Figure 1.7 (p. 12) shows two versions of the same text — one set in Times New Roman, which is appropriate for an academic setting, and the other set in Comic Sans MS, which generally is not. In academic or other serious writing, stick with standard fonts that are familiar to readers and that set a professional tone. (For more on typefaces in visual images, see pp. 43–44.)

Italics.   When you *italicize* a word or a passage, you call the reader's attention to it.

- Use italics for book, film, or software titles.
    My favorite novel is *Wuthering Heights.*
- Use italics for foreign words.
    My Finnish grandmother called me *Kultani* ("my golden one").
- Use italics for a technical or scientific term the first time you use it, and also provide a definition for the reader. After that, use regular type without emphasis.
    AIDS patients monitor their levels of *helper T-cells* because these cells detect antigens in the body and activate other cells to fight the antigens.

Times New Roman	**Comic Sans MS**
Does Heightened Surveillance Make Us More or Less Secure?	**Does Heightened Surveillance Make Us More or Less Secure?**
Since the terrorist attacks of September 11, 2001, a wide-ranging debate has ensued over whether face-recognition systems and other surveillance tools should be used to identify potential terrorists. While proponents see these tools as an essential defense when loosely organized terrorist cells might strike at any time, opponents say these systems are flawed at best and jeopardize the civil liberties of all citizens.	Since the terrorist attacks of September 11, 2001, a wide-ranging debate has ensued over whether face-recognition systems and other surveillance tools should be used to identify potential terrorists. While proponents see these tools as an essential defense when loosely organized terrorist "cells" might strike at any time, opponents say these systems are flawed at best and jeopardize the civil liberties of all citizens.

FIGURE 1.7   *Identical text set in two fonts*
Sources: See Figure 1.11

Because HIV destroys helper T-cells, this information indicates the status of a patient's immune system.

In a text, *italicized words* appear lighter in weight than nonitalicized words. This lightness, coupled with the slant of the letters, makes italics unsuitable for sustained reading. Use italics for emphasis, not for large blocks of text.

Boldface.   Boldface type is suitable for emphasis only. Too much boldface produces the "raisin bread" effect, a random scattering of dark spots across a light page, illustrated in Figure 1.8. Because this random scattering of boldface encourages the reader to "hear" the words as emphasized, it creates a choppy and unnatural rhythm.

Many teachers expect you to choose emphatic words, not to rely on boldface type for emphasis in academic papers. In other documents, be selective about using boldface, highlighting only words that you want the

---

Treating Carpal Tunnel Syndrome

Physicians **generally** suggest one of **three** methods of treating patients with carpal tunnel syndrome. **First,** reducing the amount of repeated **wrist** movement **can** allow the median nerve to heal. **This** can be accomplished by changing habits or **positions** or by using a wrist **splint.** . . .

FIGURE 1.8   *The raisin-bread effect produced by too much boldface*

reader to see or "hear" with emphasis added. In general, reserve boldface type primarily for headings, for key points in a list of reasons or factors, or for other similar uses.

Longevity.   People are living longer today, so Social Security funds need to stretch to accommodate these longer lives.

Inflation.   Dollars paid into the system in 1980 are not worth as much today, and interest on the fund has not kept pace with the growing need for the dollars.

PREPARING LISTS

The organization or placement of material on a page—its layout—can make information more accessible for readers. For example, lists are easier to read when they are displayed rather than integrated.

INTEGRATED LIST   Movies are rated by the film-rating board of the Classification and Rating Administration (CARA) based on several criteria, including these: overall theme, use of language, presence of violence, presence of nudity and sexual content, and combined use of these elements in the context of an individual film.

DISPLAYED LIST   Movies are rated by the film-rating board of the Classification and Rating Administration (CARA) based on several criteria, including these:
- overall theme
- use of language
- presence of violence
- presence of nudity and sexual content
- combined use of these elements in the context of an individual film

Bulleted List.   One type of displayed list uses a mark called a *bullet* to set off a fragment of information. The most common bullet is the small round one often available in a word processor's bulleted list function (•).

Use a bulleted list to enumerate steps, reasons, or items, especially when the order isn't significant, as in this example:

Controversy surrounding the 2000 presidential election climaxed in Florida, where several balloting issues converged.

- A controversial Palm Beach County ballot was blamed for several thousand votes possibly cast in error for a third-party candidate, Pat Buchanan.

- A Florida law triggered a statewide ballot recount when the votes for the two main candidates were separated by less than 1 percent.

- Outstanding absentee ballots had to be counted to determine which candidate had received the most votes.

As Figures 1.9 and 1.10 show, bullets can also effectively highlight skills or titles in a résumé, making it easier for readers to spot a job applicant's relevant experience. These résumés also illustrate effective use of boldface type as well as white space and headings, which are discussed next.

FIGURE 1.9   *Résumé for the Web*

Anne Cahill

Objective: **Position as a Registered Nurse in pediatric hospital setting**

- Education
- Experience
- Other Activities
- References
- Contact Me

Profile

New nursing graduate combines proficiency in the latest nursing techniques with significant clinical experience

- Experienced in providing professional, compassionate health-care services to children, others

- Able to work proficiently and productively in hospital settings

- Accustomed to working in a team with a broad range of health professionals and administrators

- Proficient with Microsoft Office, Database, and Windows 2000 applications and with Internet research

FIGURE 1.10   *Conventional résumé*

Anne Cahill
402 Pigeon Hill Road
Windsor, CT 06095
(860) 555-5763
acahill783@yahoo.com

Objective	Position as Registered Nurse in pediatric hospital setting
Education	**University of Connecticut,** Storrs, CT. Bachelor of Science, Major in nursing, May 2003. GPA: 3.5.
	Manchester Community Technical College, Manchester, CT. Associate degree in occupational therapy, May 1998. GPA: 3.3.
Work Experience *9/98–present*	**Certified Occupational Therapy Assistant,** Johnson Memorial Hospital, Stafford Springs, CT • Assist children with delayed motor development and cerebral palsy to develop skills for the activities of daily life
9/96–9/98	**Nursing Assistant,** Woodlake Healthcare Center, Tolland, CT • Helped geriatric residents with activities of daily living • Assisted nursing staff in treating acute-care patients
9/94–9/96	**Cashier,** Stop and Shop Supermarket, Vernon, CT • Trained newly hired cashiers
Clinical Internships	**St. Francis Hospital,** Hartford, CT • Student Nurse, Maternity and Postpartum, spring 2003 **Hartford Hospital,** Hartford, CT • Student Nurse, Pediatrics, fall 2002 **Visiting Nurse and Community Health,** Mansfield, CT • Student Nurse, Community, spring 2002 **Manchester General Hospital,** Manchester, CT • Student Nurse, Medical-Surgical, fall 2001
Computer Skills	• Proficient with Microsoft Office, Database, and Windows 2000 applications • Experienced with Internet research
Activities	• Student Union Board of Governors, University of Connecticut, class representative • Intramural soccer
References	Available upon request

Figure 1.10 shows a traditional, printed résumé. By contrast, Figure 1.9 shows the main page of a Web résumé, designed for the conventions of that medium. For example, the main page includes only what will fit legibly on a single screen. The job seeker summarizes her skills in a "profile" intended to hook prospective employers. Links to details on her education, experience, and so on are provided through the menu on the left side.

Numbered List.   Another type of displayed list, the numbered list, can emphasize the importance of sequence, especially in activity plans, how-to advice, instructional writing, or other process descriptions. Here is a simplified sequence of activities for making an article of clothing:

1. Select your pattern and fabric.
2. Lay out the pattern and pin it to the fabric, paying careful attention to the arrows and grain lines.
3. Cut out the fabric pieces following the outline of the pattern.
4. Sew the garment together using the pattern's step-by-step instructions.

USING WHITE SPACE STRATEGICALLY

White space is just that: space within a document that is free of text. Areas of blank space give the eye a rest and can frame important information. As a design device, white space allows you to increase emphasis as you guide the reader through your document. (For more about white space in visual images, see p. 40.)

College Papers.   If you have already written college papers, you have probably used white space to assist your readers. (For sample pages from an academic paper, see p. 3.) For example, one-inch margins and double spacing provide some respite for the reader's eyes. When you indent the first line of all your paragraphs, the extra white space helps the reader immediately differentiate one paragraph from the next.

Indenting an extended "block" quotation sets it off and marks it as a special kind of text. As you can see in Figure 1.11, white space is crucial to the appearance of your papers. Were this example single-spaced, it would be much too cramped. Besides interfering with readers' ability to keep their place in the text, closely spaced lines without white space might intimidate readers. When text elements are close together and look fairly uniform, readers may feel as if they are trying to merge onto a congested freeway. Some may give up if they don't see openings where they can easily jump in and begin to navigate the text.

However, if you simply separate sections of your paper by hitting the enter key an extra time or two — especially if your paper is double-spaced — you will add too much white space between sections. Extra space may create

FIGURE 1.11   *Example of double-spaced text*
Sources: "'Big Brother' Is No Longer a Fiction, ACLU Warns in New Report," American Civil Liberties Union, 15 January 2003, 23 June 2003, www.aclu.org/Privacy/Privacy.cfm?ID=11612. "Law, Order, and Terrorism: Other Nations' Remedies," Dahlia Lithwick, Slate, 5 October 2001, 23 June 2003, www.slate.msn.com/id/116673.

Does Heightened Surveillance Make Us More or Less Secure?

Since the terrorist attacks of September 11, 2001, a wide-ranging debate has ensued over whether face-recognition systems and other surveillance tools should be used to identify potential terrorists. While proponents see these tools as an essential defense when loosely organized terrorist "cells" might strike at any time, opponents say these systems are flawed at best and jeopardize the civil liberties of all citizens.

Barry Steinhardt, director of the Technology and Liberty Program of the American Civil Liberties Union, sees a clear threat to personal freedom:

Many people still do not grasp that Big Brother surveillance is no longer the stuff of books and movies.... Given the capabilities of today's technology, the only thing protecting us from a full-fledged surveillance society are the legal and political institutions we have inherited as Americans. Unfortunately, the September 11 attacks have led some to embrace the fallacy that weakening the Constitution will strengthen America. (" 'Big Brother' ")

However, others argue that technology can make us safer—and, in fact, already has. Video monitoring systems using closed-circuit televisions have been in use for years in such places as the United Kingdom, where officials say that crime has declined significantly as a result ("Law, Order, and Terrorism").

Annotations:
Centered title with space on both sides

Readable double-spaced lines

Text framed by margins

Indented paragraph

Extended quotation indented as a block

a gap that interferes with your readers' perception of your paper as a cohesive unit. This trapped white space functions only to prevent the reader's eye from making natural connections within the text.

Visuals.   Effect ve use of space is also important in visuals — such as transparencies or *PowerPoint* slides — for presentations. Providing ample space and limiting the text on each slide helps readers absorb the major points you want to make. For example, the first slide in Figure 1.12 contains too much text, making it hard to read and potentially distracting for the audience. In contrast, Figure 1.13 contains less text and more open space, making each point easier to read. It also uses bullets effectively to highlight the main points. These points are meant only to summarize major issues and themes, not to detail all of them; you can flesh out your main points during your talk. Additionally, though the slides have been reduced to fit in this booklet, the original type sizes were large enough to be viewed by the presenter's classmates: 44 points for the heading and 32 points for the body.

Finally, as you can see, the "white space" without text in these slides is actually blue. Some public-speaking experts believe that black type on a white background can be too stark for a slide; instead, they recommend using a dark blue background with yellow or white type. However, others believe that black on white is fine and may in fact be what the audience is accustomed to. Presentation software like *PowerPoint* makes it easy for you to experiment with these options.

USING HEADINGS AND ALIGNMENT

Readers of both texts and visuals look for cues about what's most important and about how various components are related to one another. Effective document design provides just such cues through features like headings and subheadings. Clear headings and subheadings help your readers navigate by showing a document's hierarchy of ideas. Appropriately aligned headings guide the reader's eye.

Heading Levels.   The relative size and prominence of the section headings indicate how a document is structured and which sections are most important. Headings also name the sections so that readers know where they are and where they are going. Though headings are often unnecessary in short essays, they can focus the attention of readers while providing a useful pathway through complex documents such as research papers, lab reports, business proposals, and Web-based documents.

Use typographical elements to distinguish clearly between levels of headings and subheadings within your document. Once you decide what a major section (or *level-one*) heading should look like — boldfaced and italicized, for example — be consistent with the comparable headings

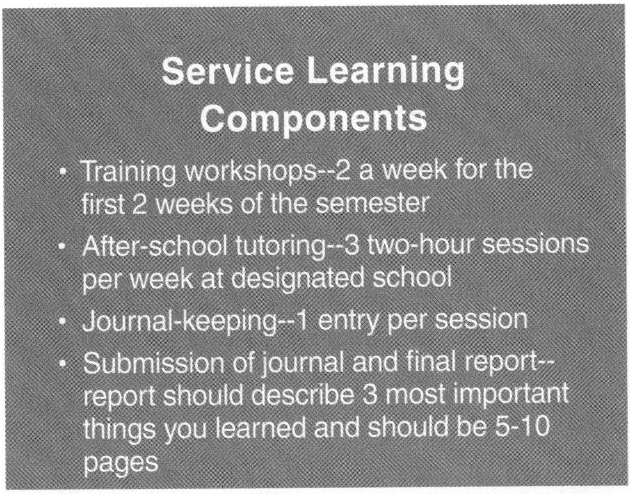

FIGURE 1.12
PowerPoint *slide with too much text and too little space*

FIGURE 1.13
PowerPoint *slide with brief text and effective use of space*

throughout your document. Treat minor headings consistently as well. In this booklet, you'll notice that all of the major headings within a chapter are set like this:

Level-One Heading   [16-point, boldfaced, italicized, in color]

Level-two and level-three headings are set like this:

LEVEL-TWO HEADING	[11.5-point, capitalized, boldfaced, in color]
Level-Three Heading	[10-point, boldfaced]

Each of these styles is used consistently in order to offer readers visual cues to both content and organization. The headings differ from each other and from the main text in size, style, and color. Differentiating headings in such ways makes your text easier to read and easier to use whether your reader is scrutinizing every word or scanning only key points.

If your instructor asks you to follow the guidelines of a particular style, you may have less flexibility in formatting headings. For example, the American Psychological Association (APA) illustrates five levels of headings, all in the same regular font style and size as the body text but varying capitalization, placement (centered or left), and underlining to distinguish the levels. MLA, however, does not recommend headings or discuss their design. (For more on MLA style, consult the *MLA Handbook for Writers of Research Papers* or go to www.mla.org/style. For more on APA style, consult the *Publication Manual of the American Psychological Association* or www.apastyle.org.)

Heading Consistency.   The headings in your document should be brief, clear, and informative. The four most common styles of headings are -*ing* phrases, noun phrases, questions, and imperative sentences. Effective writers maintain consistent parallel phrasing, whatever the style they choose. In other words, if you write a level-one heading as an -*ing* phrase, make certain that all of the level-one headings that follow are also -*ing* phrases.

Here are some examples of each style of heading:

-*ING* PHRASES
Using the College Catalog
Choosing Courses
Declaring a Major

NOUN PHRASES
The Benefits of Electronic Commerce
The Challenges of Electronic Commerce
The Characteristics of the E-Consumer

QUESTIONS
What Is Hepatitis C?
Who Is at Risk?
How Is Hepatitis C Treated?

IMPERATIVE SENTENCES
Initiate Your IRA Rollover
Learn Your Distribution Options
Select New Investments

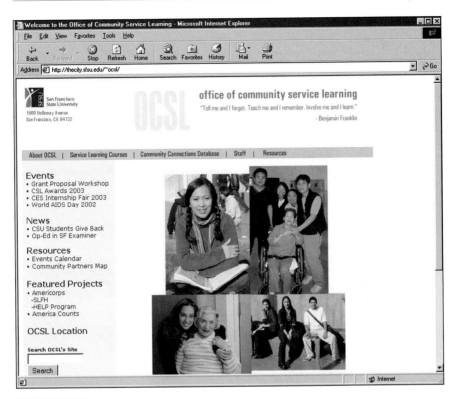

FIGURE 1.14   *Parallel headings on a Web page*
Source: Office of Service Learning, San Francisco State University

The Web page shown in Figure 1.14 uses nouns and noun phrases (for example, Events, News, Resources, Featured Projects, and OCSL Location) as headings. Under the headings are links to other content at the site, listed in a comparable fashion. In general, Web pages — especially home pages and site guides — tend to have more headings than other types of documents because they are designed to help readers find information quickly, within a small viewing frame. If you are designing a Web page, consider what different users might want to find on your site, and clearly connect your headings and content to users' needs. (For more information on Web design, visit the Web Style Guide at www.webstyleguide.com.)

Heading Alignment.   Besides being consistently styled and phrased, headings should also be consistently placed, or aligned, along the same vertical line. Figure 1.15 (p. 22) illustrates confusing alignment: the text in the top section is left aligned; the text in the middle section is right aligned; and the text in the bottom section runs out to both the left and right margins (in other words, it is fully justified). Because your title is generally centered, you might be tempted to center all of your headings, but doing so may introduce nonfunctional white

FIGURE 1.15   *Centered title over text with varying alignments*

Source: "The Progressive Party Platform of 1912." From National Party Platforms 1840–1964. *Kirk H. Porter and Donald Bruce Johnson, comps. U of Illinois P., 1966, 175–78.*

The Progressive Party Platform of 1912

The Rule of the People

The National Progressive party, committed to the principles of government by a self-controlled democracy expressing its will through representatives of the people, pledges itself to secure such alterations in the fundamental law of the several States and the United States as shall insure the representative character of the government.

In particular, the party declares for direct primaries for the nomination of State and National officers; for nationwide preferential primaries for candidates for presidency; for the direct election of the United States Senators by the people; and we urge on the States the policy of the short ballot, with responsibility to the people secured by the initiative, referendum and recall.

Amendment of Constitution

The Progressive party, believing that a free people should have the power from time to time to amend their fundamental law so as to adapt it progressively to the changing needs of the people, pledges itself to provide a more easy and expeditious method of amending the Federal Constitution. . . .

Equal Suffrage

The Progressive party, believing that no people can justly claim to be a true democracy which denies political rights on account of sex, pledges itself to the task of securing equal suffrage to men and women alike.

---

space that detracts from the effectiveness of your paper. Instead, rely on the graphic designer's principle of alignment: each element should be aligned with at least one other item, rather than having an alignment all its own.

But centering *is* an alignment, you might protest. Indeed, centering all of your headings and subheadings should create a uniform alignment throughout your paper. Except in cases of coincidence, however, each centered heading will be a different length and thus will have a different alignment, as you can see in Figure 1.16.

In contrast, in Figure 1.17 the headings are positioned at the left margin (or "flush left," as the designers call it) to create a strong line down the left side of the page. This line helps keep the reader's eye moving downward and forward through the paper. The indented paragraphs also line up with each other, creating another strong alignment on the page. The text itself lines up along the left margin. The Web page in Figure 1.14 also aligns the headings in its menu.

Much of the time you will use both left-aligned text and left-aligned headings in your document. Right-aligned text is rare in a college paper, except for special elements such as running headers and footers (discussed on p. 24). Some people like the tidy look of fully justified text, but you should use it with caution. The computer justifies text by adding extra white space between words and by hyphenating words that don't fit on a line; both of these tech-

FIGURE 1.16   *Centered headings (no strong alignment)*

The Progressive Party Platform of 1912

The Rule of the People

The National Progressive party, committed to the principles of government by a self-controlled democracy expressing its will through representatives of the people, pledges itself to secure such alterations in the fundamental law of the several States and the United States as shall insure the representative character of the government.

In particular, the party declares for direct primaries for the nomination of State and National officers; for nationwide preferential primaries for candidates for presidency; for the direct election of the United States Senators by the people; and we urge on the States the policy of the short ballot, with responsibility to the people secured by the initiative, referendum and recall.

Amendment of Constitution

The Progressive party, believing that a free people should have the power from time to time to amend their fundamental law so as to adapt it progressively to the changing needs of the people, pledges itself to provide a more easy and expeditious method of amending the Federal Constitution. . . .

Equal Suffrage

The Progressive party, believing that no people can justly claim to be a true democracy which denies political rights on account of sex, pledges itself to the task of securing equal suffrage to men and women alike.

FIGURE 1.17   *Left-aligned title, headings, and text (strong alignment)*

The Progressive Party Platform of 1912

The Rule of the People

The National Progressive party, committed to the principles of government by a self-controlled democracy expressing its will through representatives of the people, pledges itself to secure such alterations in the fundamental law of the several States and the United States as shall insure the representative character of the government.

In particular, the party declares for direct primaries for the nomination of State and National officers; for nationwide preferential primaries for candidates for presidency; for the direct election of the United States Senators by the people; and we urge on the States the policy of the short ballot, with responsibility to the people secured by the initiative, referendum and recall.

Amendment of Constitution

The Progressive party, believing that a free people should have the power from time to time to amend their fundamental law so as to adapt it progressively to the changing needs of the people, pledges itself to provide a more easy and expeditious method of amending the Federal Constitution. . . .

Equal Suffrage

The Progressive party, believing that no people can justly claim to be a true democracy which denies political rights on account of sex, pledges itself to the task of securing equal suffrage to men and women alike.

---

niques make text more difficult to read. Many teachers prefer left alignment only and no automatic hyphenation, as the MLA and APA guidelines advise.

USING REPETITION PURPOSEFULLY

Though common in poetry and in technical writing, too much verbal repetition may be frowned upon in academic writing. *Visual* repetition, however, can be helpful to a reader. If you were driving along a freeway and the familiar navigation signs — the green and white rectangles — suddenly changed to purple triangles, you might wonder whether you had strayed into a different country. Similarly, if the font or alignment suddenly changes in a paper, the reader immediately asks: What is this new navigational cue? What am I expected to do now?

To avoid disorienting readers, you can repeat one or two fonts throughout your paper to sustain a clean and uncluttered look. Consistent headings and subheadings also serve as a kind of road map to guide the readers' progress. Another simple design strategy is the use of running, or repeated, headers and footers. A *running header* is a line of information that appears consistently at the top of each page of your document, while a *running footer* appears consistently at the bottom of each page. Check the top of this page and the few after it or before it to figure out the pattern for this booklet's running headers. As part of either the header or the footer, writers sometimes include information such as the document title, its file name, or a distinctive graphic. Once you create a header or footer, your word processor can automatically insert it on each page with the page number, if you've selected that option, or with the date. Figure 1.18 illustrates the type of header required in MLA style.

USING COLOR EFFECTIVELY

Until recently, college papers typically have not included much color. However, word-processing software and other programs now make it possible to include color graphics, photographs, and other images in papers. Make sure that color serves a purpose — for instance, to highlight key information — instead of being used merely as decoration. For example, a good use of color would be to distinguish the slices in a pie chart (see p. 28).

If you are creating documents beyond college papers, you may have even more opportunities to use color. For example, on a Web page you can

FIGURE 1.18   *Sample header (running head) in MLA style*

Fallon 2

Claremont's third message is that activism is needed to combat this terrorism and hatred, and he provides clear models for activism. . . .

FIGURE 1.19   *Use of color on a Web page*
Source: The Smithsonian Institution

Colorful images draw the eye
and point out key events

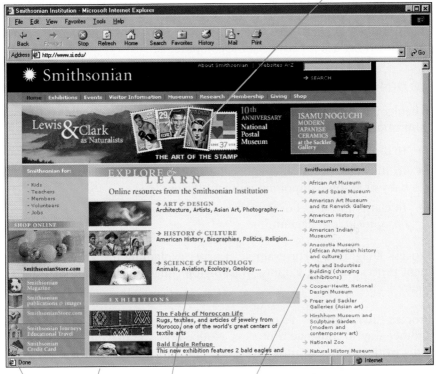

Blue headers indicate links to various museums

Green headers indicate online sources at the Smithsonian

Additional color images illlustrate links

use color to highlight headings and other key information, as Figure 1.19 shows. On any given page — in Web sites or paper documents — avoid using too many different colors because they can overload readers and defeat the purpose of helping them find important information. Also, choose your colors carefully. For example, although yellow is an attention-getting color, as school buses and traffic signs illustrate, words written in yellow on a white background are difficult to read.

Using Visuals to Reinforce Your Content

Some documents that you write may benefit from the addition of graphs, diagrams, maps, photographs, or other materials that add visual interest, convey information, and reinforce the content in your text. You might prepare these yourself or incorporate such materials from other sources, giving credit and requesting permission, if needed (see p. 29). In either case, visual materials should be appropriate for your purpose and your audience, not used as decoration. Check your software for special tools for creating graphics like pie charts, bar charts, and tables. If you are unfamiliar with these functions, ask for advice at the computer lab.

ADDING VISUALS

When could your document benefit from visuals? To answer this question, think about the ways in which visual material can support your point.

- To discuss a conflict in a certain geographical area, supply a map.
- To illustrate an autobiographical essay, scan an image of yourself as a baby or at some important moment in your life.
- To clarify the stages or steps in a process, a procedure, or a set of directions, include a diagram.

Process Diagrams.   For example, a paper explaining the wastewater treatment process in King County, Washington, might include the diagram in Figure 1.20.

Process Illustrations.   Figure 1.21, from an illustrated encyclopedia, shows another way to illustrate a process. Notice how the drawings and descriptions work together to provide an overview of the work that is done at an archaeological site.

FIGURE 1.20   *A diagram showing the process of wastewater treatment in King County, Washington*
Source: King County, Washington, Department of Natural Resources Wastewater Treatment Division
dnr.metrokc.gov/wtd/ntf/link.htm

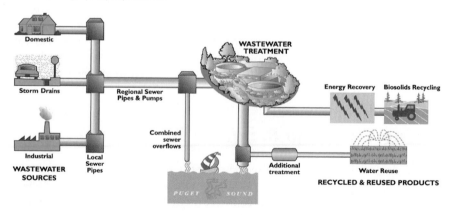

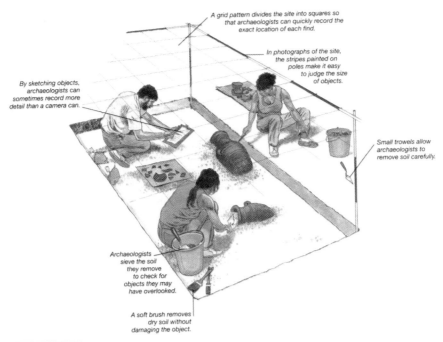

A grid pattern divides the site into squares so that archaeologists can quickly record the exact location of each find.

In photographs of the site, the stripes painted on poles make it easy to judge the size of objects.

By sketching objects, archaeologists can sometimes record more detail than a camera can.

Small trowels allow archaeologists to remove soil carefully.

Archaeologists sieve the soil they remove to check for objects they may have overlooked.

A soft brush removes dry soil without damaging the object.

FIGURE 1.21   *Illustration of work at an archaeological dig*
Source: *Dorling Kindersley* Children's Illustrated Encyclopedia

Comparative Graphs and Charts.   Graphics in college papers, magazines, Web sites, and other publications also consolidate information — both numbers and words — in visual form.

- To illustrate a trend or relationship — the number of school-aged children who use the Internet or the ratio of men to women at your college — create a graph in a spreadsheet and include it in your paper.
- To illustrate percentages or shares of a whole, add a pie chart.
- To compare various values or amounts, provide a bar chart.

For example, a graph like the one in Figure 1.22 (p. 28) can show a trend or emphasize a contrast.

To illustrate percentages or shares of a whole, consider using a pie chart, such as the one in Figure 1.23 (p. 28). This chart, shown with the brief article that it illustrates, indicates how much of the total (100%) "standby energy" various types of appliances use. Notice how color is also used to distinguish the "slices" of the pie.

To compare various values or amounts, you might want to include a bar chart like the one in Figure 1.24 (p. 28). This chart, used to illustrate an article about increased driving restrictions for teens, supplies an at-a-glance comparison of the number of car crashes occurring in various age groups.

Regional Residential Heating Oil Prices

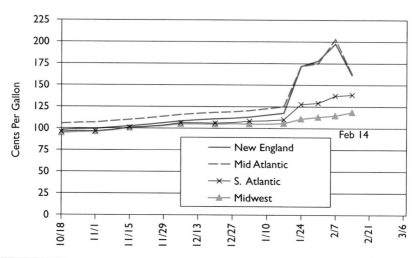

FIGURE 1.22   *A graph showing prices for residential heating oil in different regions from October 1999 to March 2000*
Source: *Energy Information Administration/State Energy Office Data* www.eia.doe.gov/pub/oil_gas/petroleum/presentations/2000/senate022400/senate022400.htm

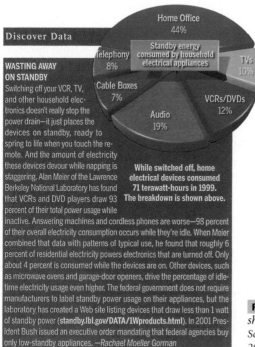

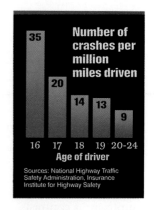

FIGURE 1.24   *A bar chart presenting numerical comparisons*
Source: U.S. News & World Report, *April 8, 2002, page 48*

FIGURE 1.23   *A pie chart showing shares of a whole*
Source: Discover *magazine, December 2002, page 13*

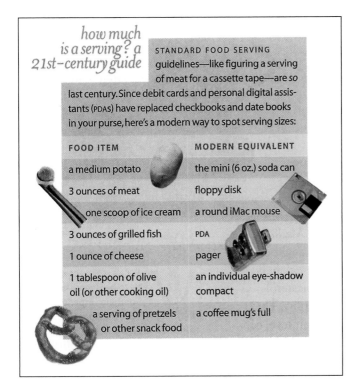

FIGURE 1.25
A table organizing textual data
Source: Health magazine, May 2002, page 35

Comparative Tables.   Consider using a table to organize textual information for easier reading. Typically, tables have columns (running up and down) and rows (running across). Tables are common in academic and workplace writing, but they are also used in popular magazines, as Figure 1.25 shows. The information in this table could have been explained in a paragraph, but a block of text would have been less accessible for readers — and far less visually interesting. Notice how the design is brought to life with the addition of little photographs of the various objects described.

Check your software for special tools for creating graphics like pie charts, bar charts, and tables. If you are unfamiliar with these functions, ask for advice at the computer lab.

CREDITING SOURCES

If you include visual materials from another source, printed or electronic, credit that source in your essay. Be sure to ask permission, if required, to use an image so that you don't risk violating the copyright. If you download an image from the Web, check the site for its guidelines for the use of images. Follow these guidelines, asking permission if necessary and giving credit to the owner of the copyright. If you are uncertain about whether you can use an image from a source, check with your teacher.

ARRANGING VISUALS AND TEXT IN YOUR DOCUMENT

Using visuals can create problems in *layout*, the arrangement of text and graphics on a page. Here are some guidelines for ensuring that your layout is effective and appropriate for your purpose and audience.

Integration of Visuals and Text. Because you are including the visual to support an idea in your text, your reader will make better sense of the graph, chart, diagram, or photograph if you provide a context for it. In an introductory sentence, you should give your reader this information:

- The number or letter of the visual (for example, Figure 6)
- Its location (on page 9, in section 3)
- Its content
- The point that it helps you to make

Also supply a label with your visual to identify its topic and number.

Placement and Alignment of Visuals. Keep your readers' needs in mind. Placing the visual close to the related discussion will make your document easier to follow. Readers can get easily distracted if they must flip from the body of your text to an appendix, for example. In addition, your headings and text are aligned at the left margin to sustain a strong forward flow through the document, you may not want to disrupt the flow by centering your visuals. Let your eye be the judge.

Balance between Visuals and Text. The visuals should support, not overshadow, the content of your paper. Try to strike a balance between the size of any single graphic or image and the related chunks of text. Though a reader's eye should be drawn to the visual, try to give it an appropriate — rather than excessive — share of the page layout.

Consider the following questions as you design your document:

DOCUMENT DESIGN CHECKLIST

____ Does your document design meet your readers' expectations and acknowledge their constraints?

____ Does your document design help to achieve your purpose, that is, your reason for writing? Does it help emphasize your key points and demonstrate a clear organization?

____ Have you used appropriate fonts, or typefaces, in your document? Do you use boldface and italic type sparingly for emphasis? Have you used displayed lists when appropriate to call out information?

____ Does the white space in your document work strategically, calling attention to or linking certain portions of text rather than creating gaps between textual elements?

___ Do your headings, subheadings, and alignment provide your reader with clear and purposeful navigational cues?

___ Have you used repeated elements, such as running headers or footers, that increase visual coherence?

___ Do your diagrams, photographs, or other illustrations clarify your content? Do your graphs, charts, or tables present numerical or textual information "at a glance"?

___ Have you used color effectively to highlight, distinguish, or organize information?

___ Does your layout integrate the visuals using appropriate placement, sizing, and alignment?

___ Have you secured any permission needed to use copyrighted material? Have you credited the source of each visual?

■ Exercises

1. Experiment with the fonts that are available on your computer. Using a paragraph or two from a recent paper, go through the font list to see how your sentences look in various fonts available to you. Test different sizes as well as the bold and italic versions. How readable is each font?

2. Look at a bulletin board, literature rack, magazine shelf, or other location where many different examples of printed material are displayed. Identify several different uses of fonts to establish a mood or convey a message. Select one example that you find particularly effective, and briefly explain how the font helps to convey the desired mood or message to the audience. If possible, include a copy of the example with your paper.

3. Using your favorite search engine (Google or Yahoo!, for example), locate an online example of a research paper or report. (The keywords "research paper" or "research report" should return several examples.) Or find a technical or government report online or in the library. Read the abstract or introduction to get an idea of the author's topic. Then quickly skim the report in order to answer the following questions:
   a. What is the purpose of the report?
   b. Who is the intended audience or reader? How can you tell?
   c. In what ways does the writer use document design strategies to address readers' needs and constraints?
   d. How does the writer use document design strategies to make his or her point?
   e. What design revisions would you recommend to the writer? How might these changes improve the reading experience of the intended audience?

   Write a brief essay presenting your findings.

4. FOR GROUP WORK: Assemble several different documents that you are reading or might read—perhaps a textbook, a newspaper, a magazine, a brochure, a catalog, or a campus publication. Examine each document carefully, considering which aspects of the design seem effective or ineffec-

tive in achieving the writer's purpose and meeting the reader's needs. Then, bring your documents and notes to class. In groups of three to five students, share your findings.

5. In a small group, examine several different documents — one supplied by each group member or one or two of the document sets prepared for group exercise 4. For each document, consider what other design choices might have made the visual presentation more effective. When you've finished your analysis, share your findings with the rest of the class.

Part 2
Strategies for Understanding Visual Representations

On a street-corner billboard, a man is biting into a jelly doughnut while driving, a look of horror on his face. He's horrified because a big blob of purple jelly (captured in midair) is about to land in the middle of his white dress shirt. The only other picture on the billboard is a detergent manufacturer's logo.

Other billboards on this corner advertise such diverse commodities as fast food, cell-phone services, and the radiology department at a local hospital. Thousands of drivers pause at this intersection to wait out a red light — a captive audience for aggressive and compelling visual representations. It's a good location for the detergent ad: drivers who pass the billboard, especially those who are eating in their cars, will relate to the problem of food spills on nice clothes. Obviously, the company that sponsored the ad hopes these people will remember its brand — the one that can tackle even the worst stains on the whitest shirts — the next time they buy laundry detergent.

The specific images on these billboards change with time, but images are a constant and persistent presence in our lives. The sign atop a taxi invites us to try the new ride at a local tourist attraction. A celebrity sporting a milk moustache smiles from the side of a city bus, accompanied by the familiar question, "Got milk?" The lettering on a pickup truck urges us to call for a free landscaping estimate. On television, video, and the Web, advertising images surround us, trying to shape our opinions about everything from personal hygiene products to snack foods to political candidates.

Advertisements are not the only visual representations that affect us. Cartoons, photographs, drawings, paintings, logos, graphics, and other two-dimensional media originate from a variety of sources with a variety of purposes — and all work to evoke responses. The critical skills you develop for analyzing these still images also apply to other types of visual representations, including television commercials, films, and stage productions. We can't help but notice visual images, and whether we respond with a smile or a frown, one thing is certain: visuals help to structure our views of reality.

Using Strategies for Visual Analysis

Begin a visual analysis by conducting a *close reading* of the image. Like a literal and critical reading of a written text, a close reading of an image involves careful, in-depth examination of the advertisement, photograph, cartoon, artwork, or other visual representation. Your close reading should focus on the following three levels of questions:

- What is the big picture? What is the source of the image? What is its purpose? What audience does it address? What prominent element in the image stands out? What focal point draws the eye?

- What characteristics of the image can you observe? What story does the image tell? What people or animals appear in the image? What are the major elements of the image? How are they arranged?

- How can you interpret what the image suggests? What feeling or mood does it create? What is its cultural meaning? What are the roles of any signs, symbols, or language that it includes? What is the image about?

Figure 2.1 reviews these three levels of visual analysis, and the rest of the chapter explains them in more detail. You may discover that your classmates respond differently to some images than you do. Your personal cultural background and your experiences may influence how you interpret the meaning of an image. If you plan to write about the image you analyze, take notes or use your journal to record your observations and interpretations. Be sure to include a copy of the image, if one is available, when you solicit

FIGURE 2.1   *Three levels of visual analysis*

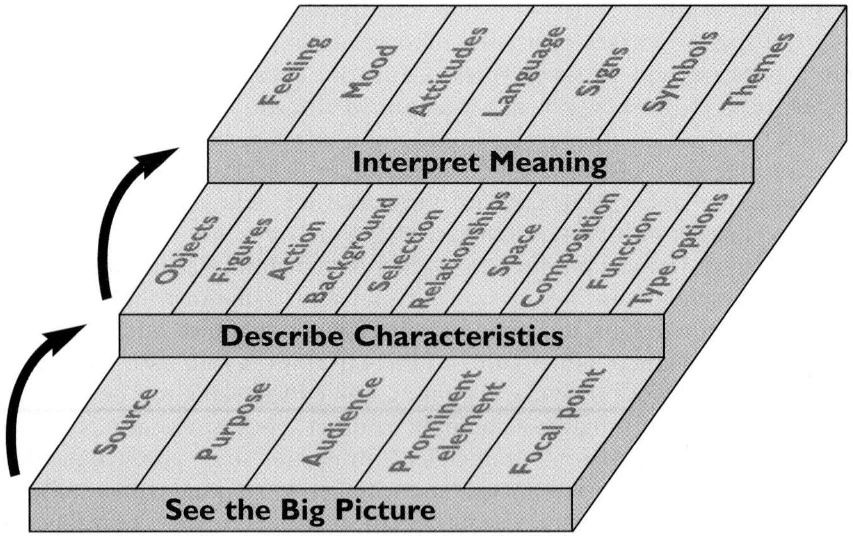

peer review of your essay or submit it to your teacher. (For a checklist for analyzing images, see p. 47.)

Level One: Seeing the Big Picture

Begin your close reading of an image by discovering what you can about its source and its overall composition. If you include the image in a paper for your class, you will need to cite the source and its "author" or artist, just as you would if you were including text from a reading, an article, or a literary work.

PURPOSE AND AUDIENCE

Identifying the purpose and intended audience for an image is sometimes complicated. For example, an image may appear in its original context or in a different situation, used seriously, humorously, or allusively. Use the following checklist to help you find out as much as you can about the purpose and audience for the image:

PURPOSE AND AUDIENCE CHECKLIST

___ What is the context for the image? For example, if it is an advertisement, when and where did it run? If it is a photograph, painting, or other work of art, who is the artist? Where has it been published or exhibited?

___ What is the purpose of the image?

___ What audience does the image aim to attract?

After considering purpose and audience, examine the overall composition of the image. The photograph in Figure 2.2 (p. 37) will serve as a guide to this process.

PROMINENT ELEMENT

Start with the overall view. Look carefully at the whole image and ask yourself, "Is there one prominent element — object, person, background, writing — in the image that immediately attracts my attention?" Examine that element in detail, and ask yourself how and why that prominent element draws you into the image.

In Figure 2.2, many people would first notice the dark-haired Caucasian girl. Her prominence in the picture can be explained in part by her position at the left side of the photograph, framed by the white porch railing. People who read from left to right and top to bottom — including most Americans and Europeans — also typically read photographs in the same way, which means that the viewer's eye is likely to be drawn into the photograph at the upper left corner. For this reason, artists and photographers often position the key elements of their photographs — the elements they want their viewers to see right away — somewhere in the upper left quadrant of the page. (See Figure 2.3, p. 37.)

FOCAL POINT

There is another reason the reader's eye might be drawn first to the girl on the left: notice that all of the other children are turned slightly toward her, straining to see the pages of the magazine she is holding. Not only is she positioned so as to provide a focal point for the viewer, but she is also the focal point of action within the photograph.

Now, take a look at the child on the right side of the picture. You may have noticed her first. Or, once you did notice her, you may have been surprised that she didn't attract your attention right away. After all, she provides some contrast within the photograph because she sits apart from the other girls, seems to be a little younger, and does not appear to be included in their little group. What's more, she's not wearing any clothes. Still, most people won't notice her first because of the path the eye typically travels within a photograph. Because of the left-to-right and top-to-bottom reading pattern that Americans and Europeans take for granted, most of us view photographs in a Z pattern, as depicted in Figure 2.4 (p. 37). Most viewers would notice the child on the far right last but would pause to look at her, observe that she's naked, and see that she's looking over at the other girls. Thus, the bottom right corner of an image becomes a second very important position that a skilled photographer can use to retain the viewers' attention. When you look at the "big picture" in this way, you can see the overall composition of the image, identify its prominent element, and determine its focal point.

Level Two: Observing the Characteristics of an Image

As you concentrate on the literal reading of a written text, you become aware of the information it presents, you comprehend what it means, and you are able to apply it in relation to other situations. Similarly, your close reading of an image includes observing its *denotative* or literal characteristics. At this stage, you focus on exactly what the image depicts — observing it objectively — rather than probing what it means or signifies.

CAST OF CHARACTERS

Objects. Examine the condition, colors, sizes, functions, and positions of the objects included in the image. In Figure 2.2, for example, only one

FIGURE 2.2 *(top)*

Photograph of four children, Kodak Picture of the Day, October 22, 2000

FIGURE 2.3 *(above left)*

Photograph divided into quarters

FIGURE 2.4 *(above right)*

Z pattern often used to read images

FIGURE 2.5 *(right)*

Close-up detail of photograph

object is depicted in the image: a large magazine. Everything else in the image is either a figure or part of the background.

Figures.   Look closely at any figures (men, women, children, animals) in the image. Consider their facial expressions, poses, hairstyles and colors, ages, sexes, ethnicity, possible education, suggested occupations, apparent relationships to each other, and so on.

Figure 2.2 shows four girls; three are about eight or nine years old, and the fourth appears to be a few years younger. Three of the girls are Caucasian, and one is African American. The dark-haired Caucasian girl is wearing a colorful bathing suit. Next to her sits a light-haired Caucasian girl, wearing shorts and a short-sleeved blue and white flowered T-shirt. The African American girl sitting beside the light-haired girl also has on a colorful print swimsuit. All three appear to be dressed appropriately for the weather. The three girls pore over the magazine held by the dark-haired Caucasian girl. Judging from their facial expressions, they are totally engrossed in the contents of the magazine, as well as a little puzzled. The girls seem to be looking at a picture; the magazine is turned sideways with the spine at the bottom.

The fourth child, the youngest in the photograph, sits slightly apart from the others. Her light hair appears damp — we might wonder if she has recently bathed or is perspiring from exertion. Because two of the other girls are attired in swimsuits, we might conclude that the youngest child's hair is damp from swimming. We can see that her skin is tanned and that she has several small bruises on her legs, probably acquired during normal play. Her right leg is crossed over her left, causing her body to turn slightly away from the other girls. Her face is turned toward them, however, and she seems to be trying to see what they are looking at. Her hands are raised, her eyes are bright, and she's smiling at whatever she is able to see of the magazine.

STORY OF THE IMAGE

Action.   The action shown in an image suggests its "plot" or story, the events surrounding the moment captured in the image. In Figure 2.2, four children are seated on the steps of a house looking at a magazine on a summer day. Because no adults appear in the picture and the children look puzzled, we might assume that they are looking at something they don't understand, possibly something adults might frown on. On the other hand, they are not acting secretive, so this impression may not be accurate.

Background.   The background in an image shows where and when the action takes place. In Figure 2.2, the children are seated on the wooden steps of a blue house. We might conclude that the steps are part of a back porch rather than a front porch because the porch is relatively small and the steps begin immediately: there is no deck and consequently nowhere to sit except on the steps themselves. The top step is painted blue, and the railing is painted white to match the white metal door and window frames. In a few places the paint is chipped or worn away. But these signs of disrepair simply seem to indicate that the house is lived in and comfortable; they are not severe enough to suggest that the occupants are poor. In the windows next to the steps and on the door, we can see the reflections of trees. The children's clothes identify the season as summer.

DESIGN AND ARRANGEMENT

Selection of Elements.   When you look at the design of an image, you might reflect on both the elements within the image and their organization.

- What are the major colors and shapes?
- How are they arranged?
- Does the image appear balanced? Are light and dark areas arranged symmetrically?
- Does the image appear organized or chaotic?
- Is one area of the picture darker (heavier) or brighter (lighter) than other areas?
- What does the design make you think of—does it evoke a particular emotion, historical period, or memory?

In Figure 2.2, the most prominent shape is the white porch railing that frames the children and draws the viewer's eye in toward the action. The image appears balanced, in that the white door provides the backdrop for the youngest child, while the blue siding and white porch railing seem to frame the other girls. Therefore, the image is split down the center, both by the division that separates the figures in the image and by the shapes that make up the background. The brightly colored summer clothing worn by the girls on the left side also accentuates the youngest child's monochromatic nakedness.

Relationship of Elements.   Visual elements may be related to one another or to written material that appears with them. As you notice such relationships, consider what they tell you. In Figure 2.2, for instance, the three older girls are grouped together around the magazine, and the youngest child is clearly not part of their group. She is separated physically from the others by a bit of intervening space and by the vertical line formed by the doorframe, which splits the background in two. She is further set apart from them by the fact that they are clothed and she is not. Moreover, her body is turned slightly away from them. However, her gaze, like the other girls', is on the magazine that they are scrutinizing; this element of the picture connects all of the children together.

Use of Space. An image may be surrounded by a lot of "white space" — empty space without text or graphics — or it may be "busy," filled with visual and written elements. White space is effective when it provides relief from an otherwise busy layout or when it directs the reader's eye to key elements of the image. The image in Figure 2.2 does not include any empty space; its shapes and colors guide the viewer's eye.

In contrast, look at the image in Figure 2.6 (p. 41). It specifically uses white space to call attention to the Volkswagen's small size. When this advertisement was produced back in 1959, many American cars were large and heavy. The VW, a German import, provided consumers with an alternative type of vehicle, and the advertising emphasized this contrast. (For more information on white space in document design, see pp. 16–18.)

ARTISTIC CHOICES

Whether an image is a photograph, a drawing, or another form of representation, the person who composes it considers its artistic effect, its function, and its connection to related text.

Composition Decisions. Aesthetic or artistic choices may vary with the preferences of the designer and the characteristics of the medium. For example, if an image is a photograph, the photographer might use a close-up, medium, or wide-angle shot to compose it — and also determine the angle of the shot, the lighting, and the use of color.

The picture of the four children in Figure 2.2 is a medium shot and has been taken at the children's eye level. If the photograph were a close-up, only one aspect of the image would be visible. Notice in Figure 2.5 how the meaning of the picture changes when we view the girls' faces as a close-up. We have no way of telling where the picture was taken or what the girls are doing; moreover, by moving in closer, this view completely cuts out the youngest child. The girls' attentiveness is still apparent, and it is clear that they are all attending to the same thing, but we can't quite tell what this thing is.

In contrast, in the Volkswagen ad (Figure 2.6), the white space creates the effect of a long shot taken from below with a telephoto lens. We see the car as it might appear if we were looking down at it through the wrong end of a pair of binoculars. This vantage point shrinks the car so that an already small vehicle looks even smaller.

Function Decisions. When using an image to illustrate a point, either alone or in connection with text, a writer must make sure that the illustration serves the overall purpose of the document; in other words, form should follow function. For example, the 1959 Oldsmobile ad, Figure 2.7 (p. 42), shows people who seem to be having a good time; in fact, one scene is set near the shore. These illustrations suggest that those who purchase the cars will enjoy life, a notion that undoubtedly suits the advertiser's goals.

FIGURE 2.6   *Volkswagen advertisement, about 1959*

Writers have many choices available to them for illustrations — not only photographs and drawings but also charts, graphs, and tables. As discussed in Part 1 of this booklet (see pp. 25–30), certain types of visuals are espe-

FIGURE 2.7   *Oldsmobile advertisement, 1959*

cially suited to certain functions. For example, a pie chart is perhaps the best way to convey parts of a whole visually. (For a sample pie chart, see Figure 1.23, p. 28.) A photograph effectively captures the drama and intensity of the moment — a child's rescue, a family's grief, or an earthquake's toll.

When you look at newspapers, magazines, and other publications, consider how the various visuals function and why the writer might have chosen to include them.

Typeface Options. Many images, especially advertisements, combine image and text, using the typeface to set a particular mood and convey a particular impression. For example, Times New Roman is a common typeface, easy to read and somewhat conservative, whereas **Comic Sans MS** is considered informal — almost playful — and looks like handwriting. Any printed element included in an image may be trendy or conservative, large or small, in relation to the image as a whole. Further, it may be meant to inform, evoke an emotion, or decorate the page. (For more on typefaces, see pp. 9–13.)

Look back at Figure 2.6, the 1959 Volkswagen ad. The words "Think small" are printed in a sans serif typeface — spare and unadorned, just like the VW itself. (For a definition and example of sans serif type, see p. 10.) The ad also includes a significant amount of text across the bottom of the page. While this text is difficult to read in the reproduction in this booklet, it humorously points out the benefits of driving a small imported vehicle instead of one of the many large, roomy cars common at the time.

In contrast to the VW ad campaign, the 1959 Oldsmobile marketing strategy promoted a big vehicle, not a small one, as Figure 2.7 illustrates. Here the cars are shown in medium to close-up view to call attention to their length. Happy human figures positioned in and beside the cars emphasize their size, and the cars are painted in bright colors, unlike the VW's serviceable black. The type in the ad, like the other visual elements, reflects and promotes the Oldsmobile's size. The primary text in the center of the page is large enough to be read in the reproduction here. It introduces the brand name by opening the first sentence with the Oldsmobile '59 logo and praises the cars' expansive size, space, power, and other features. Near the bottom of each car image, however, are a few lines of "fine print" that are difficult to read in the reproduction — brief notes about other features of the car.

Other images besides advertisements use type to evoke a mood. For example, Figures 2.8 and 2.9 (p. 44) use type alone to set a mood or convey feelings and ideas. Figure 2.8 is a design student's response to an assignment that called for using letters to create an image. The student used a simple typeface and a stairlike arrangement to help viewers "experience" the word *stairway.* Figure 2.9 illustrates how certain typefaces have become associated with particular countries — even to the point of becoming clichés. In fact, designers of travel posters, travel brochures, and other such publications often draw on predictable typographical choices like these to suggest a feeling or mood — for example, boldness, tradition, adventure, history.

Just as type can establish a mood or tone, the absence of any written language in an image can also affect how we view that image. Recall Figure 2.2, the photograph of the children sitting on the porch looking at a magazine. Because we can't see the magazine's title, we are left to wonder —

s
st
sta
stair
stairw
stairwa
stairway

FIGURE 2.8   *Artistic use of type*
Source: Design for Communication:
Conceptual Graphic Design Basics

GREECE
JAMAICA
Ceylon
China
MEXICO
Tahiti
Canada
Ireland
Scotland
Denmark
Japan
PORTUGAL
BRITAIN

FIGURE 2.9   *Type as cultural cliché*
Source: Publication Design

perhaps with amusement—about what has so engrossed the children. If the title of the magazine—*Sports Illustrated, Wired, People*—were revealed to us, the photograph might seem less intriguing. By leaving us to speculate about the identity of the magazine, the photographer may keep us looking longer and harder at the image.

Level Three: Interpreting the Meaning of an Image

When you read a written text on an analytical level, you engage actively with the text. You analyze its parts from different angles, synthesize the material by combining it with related information, and finally evaluate or judge its significance. When you interpret an image, you do much the same, actively questioning and examining what the image *connotes* or suggests, speculating about what it signifies.

Because interpretation is more personal than observation, this process can reveal deep-seated individual and cultural values. In fact, interpreting an image is sometimes emotional or difficult because it may require you to examine beliefs that you are unaware of holding. You may even become impatient with visual analysis, perhaps feeling that too much is being read into the image. Like learning to read critically, however, learning to interpret images is a valuable skill. When you see an image that attracts you, chances are good that you like it because it upholds strong cultural beliefs. Through close reading of images, you can examine how image makers are able to perpetuate such cultural values and speculate about why—perhaps analyzing an artist's political motivations or an advertiser's economic motivations. When you interpret an image, you go beyond literal observation to examine what the image suggests and what it may mean. (For a checklist for analyzing images, see p. 47.)

GENERAL FEELING OR MOOD

To begin interpreting an image, consider what feeling or mood it creates and how it does so. If you are a woman, you probably recall huddling, around age eight or nine, with a couple of "best friends" as the girls do in Figure 2.2. As a result, the interaction in this photograph may seem very familiar and may evoke fond memories. If you are a man, this photograph may call up somewhat different memories. Although eight-year-old boys also cluster in small groups, their motivations may differ from those behind little girls' huddles. Moreover, anyone who was ignored or excluded at a young age may feel a rush of sympathy for the youngest child; her separation from the older children may dredge up age-old hurt feelings.

For many viewers, the image may also suggest a mood associated with summer: sitting on the back porch after a trip to the swimming pool, spending a carefree day with friends. This "summer" mood is a particular cultural association related to the summers of childhood. By the time we reach college, summer no longer has the same feeling. Work, summer school, separations, and family responsibilities—maybe even for children like those in the picture—obliterate the freedoms of childhood summer vacations.

SOCIOLOGICAL, POLITICAL, ECONOMIC, OR CULTURAL ATTITUDES

On the surface, the Volkswagen ad in Figure 2.6 is simply an attempt to sell a car. But its message might be interpreted to mean "scale down"—lead a less consumer-oriented lifestyle. If Volkswagen had distributed this ad in the 1970s, it would have been unremarkable—faced with the first energy crisis that adversely affected American gasoline prices, many advertisers used ecological consciousness to sell cars. In 1959, however, energy conservation was not really a concern. Contrasted with other automobile ads of its time, the Volkswagen ad seems somewhat eccentric, making the novel suggestion that larger cars are excessively extravagant.

Whereas the Volkswagen ad suggests that "small" refers both to size and affordability, the Oldsmobile ad in Figure 2.7 depicts a large vehicle and implies a large price tag. By emphasizing the Vista-Panoramic view and increased luggage space and by portraying the car near a seashore, the ad leads viewers to think about going on vacation. It thus implies luxury and exclusivity—not everyone can afford this car or the activities it suggests.

Sometimes, what is missing from an image is as important as what is included. Viewers of today might readily notice the absence of people of color in the 1959 Oldsmobile ad. An interesting study might investigate what types of magazines originally carried this ad and whether (and if so, how) Oldsmobiles were also advertised in publications aimed at Asian Americans, African Americans, or Spanish-speaking people.

LANGUAGE

Just as you would examine figures, colors, and shapes when you observe the literal characteristics of an image, so you need to examine its words, phrases, and sentences when you interpret what it suggests. Does its language provide information, generate an emotional response, or do both? Do its words repeat a sound or concept, signal a comparison (such as a "new, improved" product), carry sexual overtones, issue a challenge, or offer a definition or philosophy of life? The words in the center of the Oldsmobile ad in Figure 2.7, for instance, are calculated to associate the car with a leisurely, affluent lifestyle. On the other hand, VW's "Think small" ad in Figure 2.6 turns compactness into a goal, a quality to be desired in a car and, by extension, in life.

Frequently advertisements employ wordplay to get their messages across. Often such ads are lighthearted, but they sometimes have a more serious tone. Consider, for example, the public-service advertisement in Figure 2.10, which was created by a graphic-design student. This ad features a play on the word *tolerance*, which is scrambled on the chalkboard so that the letters in the center read *learn*. The chalkboard, a typical feature of the classroom, suggests that tolerance is a basic lesson to be learned. Also, the definition of tolerance at the bottom of the ad is much like other definitions students might look up in a dictionary. (It reads, "The capacity for, or practice of, recognizing or respecting the behavior, beliefs, opinions, practices, or rights of others, whether agreeing with them or not.")

FIGURE 2.10 *Public-service advertisement showing wordplay*
Source: Design for Communication: Conceptual Graphic Design Basics

SIGNS AND SYMBOLS

Signs and symbols, such as product logos, are images or words that communicate key messages. In the Oldsmobile ad in Figure 2.7, the product logo doubles as the phrase that introduces the description of the 1959 model. Sometimes a product logo alone may be enough, as in the Hershey chocolate company's holiday ads that include little more than a single Hershey's Kiss. The shape of the Kiss serves as a logo or symbol for the company.

If you look back at the second magazine spread in Figure 1.3 (see p. 5), you'll see a prominent symbol — the U.S. flag. The flag is held by a little boy who is sitting on a man's shoulders. (Presumably, the man is the boy's father.) In this spread, the flag is associated not only with the Fourth of July, the article's subject, but also with a family's values. Even without the headings and quotations, the symbolism comes across clearly.

THEMES

The theme of an image is not the same as its plot. When you identify the plot, you identify the story that is told by the image. When you identify the theme, on the other hand, you explain what the image is about. An ad for a diamond ring may tell the story of a man surprising his wife with a ring on their twenty-fifth wedding anniversary, but the advertisement's theme could be sex, romance, longevity, or some other concept. Similarly, the theme of a soft-drink ad might be competition, community, compassion, or individualism. A painting of the ocean might be about cheerfulness, fear, or loneliness. Through a close reading, you can unearth clues and details to support your interpretation of the theme and convince others of its merit.

Ask the following questions as you analyze an image or as you prepare to present your analysis in an essay:

VISUAL ANALYSIS CHECKLIST

Seeing the Big Picture

____ What is the source of the image? What is its purpose and audience?

____ What prominent element in the image immediately attracts your attention? How and why does it draw you into the image?

____ What is the focal point of the image? How do the elements of the image direct your attention to this point? What path does your eye follow as you observe the image?

Observing the Characteristics of an Image

____ What objects are included in the image?

____ What figures (people or animals) appear in the image?

____ What action takes place in the image? What is its "plot" or story?

____ What is in the background of the image? Where does the action of the image take place? What kind of place is it?

____ What elements contribute to the design of the image? What colors and shapes does it include? How are they arranged or balanced? What feeling, memory, or association does the design evoke?

___ How are the pictorial elements related to one another? How are they related to any written material? What do these relationships tell you as a
viewer?

___ How does the image use space? Does it include a lot of white space, or
does it seem cluttered and busy?

___ What composition decisions has the designer or artist made? What type
of shot, shot angle, lighting, or color is used?

___ What is the function of the image? How does its form support its function?

___ What typefaces are used? What impressions do they convey?

Interpreting the Meaning of an Image

___ What general feeling do you get from looking at the image? What mood
does the image create? How does it create this mood?

___ What sociological, political, economic, or cultural attitudes are reflected
in the image?

___ What language is included in the image? How does the language function?

___ What signs and symbols can you identify? What role do these play in the
image?

___ What theme or themes can you identify in the image?

■ Exercises

1. Find a print ad that evokes a strong emotional response. Conduct a close
   reading of the ad, observing its characteristics and interpreting its meaning. Write an essay in which you explain the techniques by which the ad
   evokes your emotional response. Include a copy of the ad with your essay,
   and consult others to determine whether they have the same response to
   the ad.

2. Volkswagen continues to produce thought-provoking advertisements like
   the one shown in Figure 2.6 on page 41. Video clips of some of the company's recent television ads can be found at www.vw.com/musicpillar/
   ads.htm. View one or two of these advertisements, considering such features as their stories or "plots"; the choice of figures, settings, and images;
   the angles from which subjects are filmed; and any text messages included.
   Based on your analysis of the ads, decide what message you think that the
   company wants to communicate about its cars. In an essay, describe this
   message and the audience that Volkswagen seems to be aiming for, and
   discuss how the artistic choices in the ads might appeal to this audience.

3. Compile a design notebook. Over the course of several weeks, collect ten
   or twelve images that appeal to you. You may wish to choose examples of
   a particular genre, or your teacher may assign a genre or theme. For example, you might select advertisements, portraits, or landscape pho-

tographs, or you might choose snack food advertisements from magazines aimed at several different audiences. On the other hand, your collection might revolve around a theme, such as friendship, competition, community, or romance. As you collect these images, "read" each one closely, and write short responses explaining your reactions to the images based on your close readings. At the end of the collection period, choose two or three images. Write an essay in which you compare or contrast them, analyzing how they illustrate the same genre, how they convey a particular theme, or how they appeal to different audiences.

4. Visit a music store, and find a CD cover whose design interests you. Make notes about design choices such as its prominent element and focal point, the use of color and imagery, and the use of typography. Based on the design, try to predict what kind of music is on the CD. If the store has CD-listening stations, try to listen to a track or two. Did the music match your expectations based on the CD design? If you were the CD designer, would you have made any different artistic choices? Write a brief essay discussing your observations, and attach a copy of the CD cover, if possible. (You might be able to print it out from the Web.) As an alternative assignment, listen to some music that's new to you, and design a CD cover for it, applying the elements described in this chapter. Describe in a brief paper the visual elements you would include in your CD cover. If you wish, include a sketch of your design for the cover, using colored pencils or markers to suggest color choices or pasting in images or type from print sources, such as magazines or newspapers.

5. FOR GROUP WORK: Select some type of image (for example, an advertisement; a visual from a magazine or image database; a CD, DVD, or video-cassette cover) and, on your own, make notes on its "literal" characteristics. (For guidance, see "Observing the Characteristics of an Image," pp. 36–44.) Then, bring your image and notes to class. In small groups of three to five students, share your images and discuss your literal readings.

6. In a small group, pick one or two of the images that the group members analyzed for exercise 5. Ask each group member, in turn, to suggest possible interpretations of the meanings of the images. (For guidance, see "Interpreting the Meaning of an Image," pp. 44–47.) What different interpretations do group members suggest? How do you account for the differences in these interpretations? Share your findings with the rest of the class.

Acknowledgments *(continued)*

Figure 1.20: Diagram courtesy of King County, Washington, Wastewater Treatment Division.

Figure 1.21: Illustration copyright © Dorling Kindersley Ltd.

Figure 1.22: Graph courtesy of the Energy Information Administration.

Figure 1.23: Graphic by Matt Zang.

Figure 1.24: Bar chart copyright © 2002 *U.S. News & World Report*, L.P. Reprinted with permission.

Figure 1.25: Table by Sara Weeks copyright © 2002 *Health®* magazine. For subscriptions please call 1-800-274-2522.

Figure 2.2: Photograph copyright © Merrilee A. Giegerich.

Figure 2.6: Advertisement courtesy of Volkswagen of America, Inc.

Figure 2.7: Oldsmobile advertisement courtesy of Leo Burnett.

Figure 2.8: Type design courtesy of Eunjin Kim, Samsung Art and Design Institute.

Figure 2.9: Type design from Roy Paul Nelson, *Publication Design* (© 1991, The McGraw-Hill Companies). Reproduced with permission from McGraw-Hill.

Figure 2.10: Public-service announcement copyright © D. Reed Monroe.